Erotic
RECKONINGS

NEW POEMS

R. Allen Shoaf

LCCN: 2011944345
ISBN 978-0-9794561-6-9

Shoaf, R. Allen
Erotic Reckonings

Published by Summerfield Publishing,
New Plains Press
P.O. Box 1946
Auburn, AL 36831-1946
Newplainspress.com

The text of this book is composed in Garamond

Composition and cover design by Emily Wilkins

So they loved as love in twain
Had the essence but in one.
Two distincts, division none—
Number there in love was slain.

"Let the Bird of Loudest Lay"
("The Phoenix and the Turtle")
William Shakespeare

OTHER WORKS BY R. ALLEN SHOAF

<u>Scholarship:</u> *Chaucer's Body and the Anxiety of Circulation in the Canterbury Tales*

Shakespeare's Theater of Likeness

Milton, Poet of Duality

<u>Poetry:</u> *Simple Rules.*

TABLE *of* CONTENTS

Erotic
RECKONINGS

If We Don't Disfigure Ourselves

I remember once when an angry,
cold-eyed woman
huffed abuse at a man we knew,
"How could he disfigure himself so!"—
the object of her scorn about six feet two
and going three-fifty, maybe four hundred pounds,
with the most beautiful round belly in front of him
like a great globe of the world
tucked away beneath his heart ….
I'm finally old enough to answer her question:
"How could he not?"
If we don't disfigure ourselves,
how will we ever be known?—
less even than insects—
with no sects to be in?

The Old Mill Bookstore

Things cease to work. Inevitable
decay, even of prodigies. The mind
touches what no eye can see and feels.

A shallow river but a sharp bend
and drop enough to drive the wheel,
once, centuries ago, before the exiles;

now, time and the rocks have returned
clarity, and a certain anguish finds release
inside the weathered timbers and water's echo.

An old footbridge repaired guides new exiles
to a tea shop on the opposing bank,
derelict farmhouse called back for now,

where civil quiet is served with cakes,
sandwiches, and improbable cream—
we sit here, knowing we will never return

but agreed to let it pass. The card
I bought, a drawing of the mill,
has drawn me back and teaches me

things cease to work. Every age
recovers what it can. Every loss,
unbearable, is somewhere noted

in stone or blood, to be discovered
not by the eye or mind but by the heart,
which stumbles upon its ancient deceits,

recorded not only in the books
that pace along the wall and pitch
but in the wattle, too, and by the webs

and on the rocks worn glassy, smooth,
and along the pathways so many have trod,
where, as usual, they betrayed each other.

The Thorn

"Some folks complain that roses have thorns.
Other folks are thankful thorns have roses."

I culture roses for pleasure and dreaming,
My garden a bed in more senses than one,
And day after day I contemplate the thorn,
A device a poet should interrogate often.

New canes erupting unfold thorns as soft
As an infant's flesh—to even such flesh
As that, harmless—which harden in a day
To razors no infant dare ever explore.

Thousands of times I've been lacerated—
Fingers, wrists, forearms, ankles, and thighs—
Have come in to wash off trellises of blood
And wonder at appetites I don't understand.

Is it possible the drop on the thorn
Is the price demanded for my revels
In the roses I coax to grace my garden—
That that I dream on also taste of me?

That that I cut, cajole, and (on occasion) curse
Have in me its rights as well? All flesh is grass
And the flower thereof is as the grass—
And the thorn it is that bears the rose.

Death's Number

The time has come to talk of the dead,
So many voices clamoring to share
The breath I still draw from the dreams we lived
During years that seem now as dark as the sea—
And as cold, if memory warms them not.
(I think best for me … my ashes aloft
Drifting down to the waves to disappear…
Here one reason I am silent so much:
To think of theirs is to imagine mine.)
Is this the lot of those who loved, wisely
Or otherwise? To be a voice of tongues
Speaking in languages each truly dead?
Each in need of an interpreter, one
Who listens as if his life depends on it?
These questions are not distractions for us
Who have wondered why death never relents
But even now takes someone else we loved
It seems was here only moments ago.
They are the questions that tease our exhaustion,
Daring us to forget, as if we could,
Or, if we did, for longer than a song—
You do remember, don't you, the song? The one
That won't let you forget? That's death's number.
You can't orphan it. Don't even try.
Its genius runs deeper than your genes,
Offspring of your coupling of hope and fear.
There are days, you'd think it plays all the time,
An air fleeing (or is it seeking?) despair,
As if very sound harbored the craft, that wood
To ferry you to liberating union
Where the wind blows as it will but will not

Purify your mind with a merciful breeze,
For this is the song that cannot be purged—
You knew them all, each one, and how are you left?
In the night-most hour, when sleep is a dream,
Do you not ask how are you left? To be
Their not-to-be and know you cannot feel—
Have not felt, these empty years too many—
Except as the ice burns their fingers, too?
Their names traverse you like glaciers retreating,
Inscribing lines incalculably fine,
The scorings inaudible to all but you,
And so you must sing, must talk of the dead—
Everyone knows the requiem's for you.

Pleasure

It makes sense:
the most sought-after object
is the least understood;
"passion" is an ancient word for *suffering*—
a glint of sunlight gold on the crest of a wave
shrinks us to a whimper for more
when we know the craft has broken apart already
forsaken not forgiven.

At the Top of Vanishing Peak

Arriving at the foot of it,
He cannot see the top. Like others
Before him, nevertheless, he begins
His ascent. He cannot remember when
The first one appeared, to the right of his leg,
Between his knee and ankle, whiter than the whitest
Egg he had ever seen, a perfect ellipsoid hovering and throbbing.
Ever upward, now slower, now faster, he clambers, breath and bone
Almost spent, when another ellipsoid, whiter, if possible, than the first
Suddenly appears on his other side, parallel to its mate,
        of identical size and shape.
Higher and higher and higher, until on either side of him
        throb and hover five ellipsoids,
Ten in all. Over the edge his left arm first and he thrusts upward
        —to the top—
And, the glint in his eyes delirious, he drags his body out onto the flat,
Success at last within his grasp. Impeccably clean, shining brightly,
In the chamber one bullet, the metal smooth against his cheek
As the barrel comes to rest in his mouth. In the moment
Of spasm, ten perfect ellipsoids unfurl, sails immense,
Like spirits, billowing over, under, around him
Until nothing remains but blue and white
Mantling the erection of Vanishing Peak.

Flights of Faith

For my grandson, Oliver Holden Shoaf

Shall an infant grow wings on an old man's back?

We hear that no one reads poetry any longer,
                       poetry should therefore keep to itself—
                       mind its own affairs,
                              such as they are.

But I'm not convinced and find I'm impatient.

Shall an infant grow wings on an old man's back?

Every cell in me knows this is what matters:
my son talks to his son who, in a month, maybe two,
will talk to his father

             and the world
for the three of us will never be the same again.

Of the same seed, three men, who never see
the sun rise alike, so the sunrise will be
always new, and most of all when the child
exclaims, "Yes, I thee it, too!"

            and the earth
beneath us never felt like such a mother
before,

        like the women who bore us,

irreducible to fantasies of utility—
too evolved to be vessels of oblivion,
the bodies in which we found the sun.

Of what arc these flights of a faith ember
of a flame dark and cold already long ago?
To what ascent do they aspire? And how?

> *The child in my old man's arms*
> *Is not immune to age's harms,*
> *But the life I feel bless my hand*
> *Is life triumphant in new-born man.*

His laughter accounts for the mystery
otherwise ineffable,
                            lilting from his belly so little
to burst over his face crinkled with glee,

sounds so sweet angels suspend original being
to listen to a melody they have never heard,
report it to the ends of space
and add it to the energy
no one can name
with which still all life expresses

                            its enormous hazard—
to believe is to be like the love you begin.

> *Scars on an old man's skin*
> *Are the scrawl of an old man's ken.*
> *Eyes so pure and diamond bright*
> *Foretell my grandson will endure the night.*

I will tell you a story, as true as I know:
"begin" has no beginning scholars can find
(preceded by the linguists' star in lexicons
you'll see it).

     And I have lived long enough to learn
why this is so.

     Raise your arm as you always do
after you clap your hands at what has pleased you—
that is the beginning of beginning, my son,
to reach for you know not what
and make of the dragon your enduring friend.

When like me you must at last lie down,
when you feel your tongue rasp your lips,
         "no more,"
remember how you laughed
when you heard me ask,
shall an infant grow wings on an old man's back?—

and fly away, my son, fly away.

About Carbon

I

Original response is like a fork in the road;
Here moral angles have no relevance:
The choice is yours and you are the choice,

Already destined but never determined.
What you like will depend on what you are like
(Mystery deeper than religion fathoms),

And your struggle through likes to what you are like
Will cost no less than knowledge of desire,
Which corrupts you until your face reflects

The text of the languishing you call your life,
Unfinished joys and agonies you cannot revise,
Beseech and pray as you will, exhausted

By the recognition you are this history,
From which the only escape is madness.

In the air you detect a scent that once

Buried your head in the cunning of love
And you took of her body all your fill,
Testing the ancients' truth, who called it poison,

Delirious the while tasting the toxic flow.
This is the origin of your response,
The experience that devoured the devourer.

II

Oblivion is no therapy. Nor
Can you cipher the cost of oblivion
(Narcotics are vermin of Narcissus,

Numbing the body more than the mind, which spasms,
One day, wilted and rotted in the mud
Of self-love that has starved even its own echo.)

We must remember. I can report to you
That memory is corrosive torture.
Guilt is an acid that does not waste

The tissue it drips on; the same amount
Always remains and endures a lifetime.
Fear the day when terrorists will induce

Guilt into the victim's mind (Or have they
Already done that?)—the end of mankind.

    A certain pitch begins to be audible.

    You've heard it before. Something in you shudders.
    It is a noise your ears cannot abide.
    It is not loud. It is not a scream.

    It is the moan of the life that suffers
    Spirit searing body, body crippling spirit,
    In saecula saeculorum. Amen. Amen.

III

We are curious chemistry, no doubt.
Mainly, carbon. About carbon we learn
That its might is in the formation of bonds.

The seeker at the fork will need to ask
If his carbon is good char, of some use
In the coming glare of terminal blindness.

"So great," noted Lucretius, "are the evils
Religion can compel men to commit."
Tantum religio potuit suadere malorum.

Yes, but in pieties now ascending, carbon
And its alchemists lack the equations
To solve for the oddratic doom of bonds:

A planet denuded of its atmosphere—
No veil to hide its shame, no fossil fuel
To power its game—loses its gods

To the void.

> *A sudden wedge of skin*
> *Flashes before your eyes and you recall*
> *How she whispered, "so sweet, so sweet,"*
>
> *As must have done, too, women without number*
> *Men then murdered and mutilated*
> *Because they are the ovens of carbon.*

IV

Mr. Reality always has an edge.
Remember? He's the one whose large, toothy smile
Is also a razor—you're bleeding out your dream

Before you know you've even been cut. Wounds, though,
Are often the threshold of original
Response, and our scars are never just

Superficial—run your finger along one
And you will feel the rhizome eloquent
(But *cave!* Some roots resemble the razor.)

> *I remember the scars of the women*
> *I've touched. I not only see them still but feel*
> *The anguish, too, beneath the lips sewn shut,*

> *Where silence and dumbness must never be*
> *Confused lest tongues more punctual than Medusa's hair*
> *Strike without warning your unconscious disdain.*

> *We spent our youth in the Age of License*
> *And, so, many of the women touched my scars, too;*
> *We did not heal each other, suffice to say,*

> *But we learned the tax Mr. Reality*
> *Levies: it is ponderous and ubiquitous,*
> *Costing not less than subservience to him.*

V

What then is imagination, we ask?
For most, it has CGI'd into vide-antasy,
Where distraction is the only distraction,

As many observe, where we ply illusions
(I would add) in the fragile wish that All
Is illusory anyway. Somehow

This doesn't work—watch a death by cancer,
Or replay your DVD of 9/11.
No. Imagination is there, the "there"

Of words, words such as we use everyday
Without, however, sensing the life in them—
Their decay is not merely our decadence,

It is also the loss of history.
Life is worthless because the worth of life
Has no word any longer to work its wonder—

"Uzi" kills as many as the machine-gun kills.
We understand that this will never change,
Nor will the chemistry that drives our murder.

> *The policeman explained to my mother*
> *How the pushers threw Will out of their car*
> *And backed it over him. She sobbed. I write.*

VI

Form is negentropic. It resists
Randomness and decay. It fabricates things.
A thing is a gathering of entities

Into an identity. A thing, to be,
Must exclude all the things that it is not.
The thing, language, however, remembers them.

Original response is to name the thing
Without un-naming the things of the thing—
How hard it is to "tell it *like* it is"!

He who knows the likeness of the thing
Is the happiest philosopher-king,
For he also knows the peregrinations

Exilic in the basin of entropy
Where exchanges smithy infinity
But never forge ecstasy a like.

> *Years later David told me Will's GI buddies*
> *Smashed the bar to pieces where the pushers*
> *Sold the smack Will learned to like in Viet Nam*

(The police had long since "closed" the case)—
Sharp in my heart the thrill of the irony
In how much they liked my brother Will.

VII

I have been writing since I can remember.
In grammar school (age seven), I edited
The class "newspaper." But no one liked

The title for it I chose, *The Memorial.*
Memory and mourning are inseparable.
Countless are the chemicals men have tried,

But no anaesthetic touches the nerve
Esthetics does—the knot intrinsicate
Of matter and memory where we mourn

Mortality as we model the motive, "I am
To die," the modality art bestows on life.
Feeling (αἴσθησις) the origin of it all.

When I was 11, Amy lived close by: Amy
Taught me what to do when she unzipped our jeans;
I quivered and writhed and could barely breathe—

Nothing the older boys crowed came within an inch.
From that moment to this I have understood
Life isn't simple, much as we wish it were

(Or bluff that it is). Life is the longing
For original response—belonging
To oneself as if as if were real.

Perfect Imperfection

One night I caught a special about chimpanzees.
A woman who had done research on a family
returned twenty years later to visit them;
as she stepped ashore their modest island,
a matriarch, ancient, wrinkled, arthritic,
hobbled up and put her arm around her neck
and gave her a kiss with tears in her eyes—
she herself could hardly keep from weeping.
Love evolves by perfect imperfection.
As I felt my own tears stinging, I realized,
for all the lies men soil their own nest with
(including the lie they alone can love),
they will not last as they were not first.

Butterfly on My Breast

I was working among my roses in the early morning
before the sweltering
that teaches life how hot it must be.
I raised up to wipe my brow
and suddenly on my breast a butterfly lighted,
a monarch about as big as the palm of my hand.

Immediately I stood still, barely breathing,
and looking down,
never lifting my head the whole time it tarried,
for I was amazed and also humbled
to see it rest from its travail
atop my left breast,
its wings pulsing slightly up and down.

I do not know by the clock
how long we were there,
but I remember that it seemed a very long time
and I was content to be so still,
happy that the wayfarer had settled on me.

When finally it lifted to fly away
I suddenly felt how much hotter the day had become
as sweat was pouring down my face, my trunk, and my arms—
even I felt for a moment weak.

The best word for my experience comes from the Latin word for *dice*—
aleatory: sheer, random luck,
for which any account in any form must alter,
in the very moment of utterance,
what it attempts to explain.

All I can say is that for a certain beat of my life
I watched the gentle flutter of a butterfly
directly over the cavity that conceals my heart,
and there I felt how random, accidental, mysterious, and inexplicable
it is.

The Story of Orpheus and Eurydice

I've made many a trip with Orpheus.
As much as he, I want to get it right—
A philologist is a lover, too.

Entries to the underworld are everywhere
(You may have to push pollution aside),
And he has no trouble finding the way,
Nor does he begrudge showing me the signs
(They have been around a very long time).

But then it becomes a different story.
Hades is not what it used to be.

I can remember a three-headed dog,
And I saw fields they call Elysian.
But these days it's mostly mutilations
And crowds enough for Hell's own parking lot.

To get anywhere you have to step on
Corpses who complain that life's unfair,
Which it certainly is, but the Big Boss
Only listens to what he wants to hear,
And, contrary to what you may have read,
He always welcomes Orpheus back,
And will, I think, until the end of time.

For desire demands despairing ascent,
A trial of faith that cannot be won:
In every union that aspires to love
Both of you know when you should have looked back.

Tribes

There's a notion rampant nowadays
that to be who you want to be
you must belong to a tribe
since this way
(how convenient!)
you'll always have someone to blame,
the other tribes
you don't belong to:
so as long as you're some X ,
you're cool
because you can tell some Y
to go to hell
or piss off
or kiss your ass,
whatever.
And don't worry
if your tribe can't seem to win;
just switch tribes:
it's really easy—try B.

Division is primordial in us:
us against them, of all against all
the everlasting war, unlimited bloodshed,
rivers choked with corpses;
nothing makes us happier than:
"Mine is bigger than his, ha ha!"
"Mine are bigger than hers, ha ha!"
And peace is *so* johnlennon
(all we are saying is leave me alone).

There once was a tribe—
they called their river Tiber—
who seized the prize
all tribes lust and vie for:
imperium sine fine, their poet called it,
"empire without end."

Though many now say
from this tribe
nothing remains
for us to learn
(after all, who cares?),
a golden bough may still be broken
(reluctant though it be to grace our greed)—
Ibi amor, ibi patria est
not only says
"There is my love, there my fatherland,"
it also means
Amor differs from *Roma*:
love is bounded, love is a bond,
love is the only tribe
that lasts forever,
and Dido's curse is with us still,
everywhere,
even in the tribe Hades guards
and fruitful, beautiful Proserpina hates.

Broken

Some things never mend: no splinters to set,
No glue and no gut, no miracle wires.

Instruments abound, some dry and some wet,
As sharp as shark's teeth, some—some, robotic pliers.

Some devices more lethal than the wound
Razor away the little good that's left.

Some hands are so docile they feel marooned
By therapies that dare to cross the cleft.

Tears empty their ducts, like rivers run dry
A season awaiting—it will not come.

Broken at a site for which none may cry,
It isn't invisible nor is it dumb.

But we can neither see it nor hear it
Since we dammed the flaw of blood in spirit.

An Idea of the Body
as Autothanatography

Habit and you turn out to be less than friends.
The moon is where it always was and the stars.

A walk over the bridge reveals a scene
I remember… from somewhere… I forget…

Which, when I recall, clouds the scene and seals
The salience irrevocably in me

Where only the poem approaches it
(If I would compare it to the moon and the stars).

We are all inadequate to our dreams.
We have no chants, magical or otherwise,

To summon the mysteries the body stores
While we busy ourselves about our lines—

Even the poem reaches just so far,
Only echoing the pleasure evoked.

Classical Romanticism

An old fat man died in Vienna
Eighteen-ninety-seven—Johannes Brahms.
Like his father he met death in his liver—
Turned yellow at the last but told his friends
His appetite remained good till near the end.
It is said that the ships on the Elbe,
When the word went out, lowered their flags
To half mast, near Hamburg, where he was born,
Which was meet and right, for he was the best
Of Germany when Germany was new.
I descend from Germans, *Schwarzwälder*,
And I feel, I admit, some pride in the three—
Bach, Beethoven, and Brahms—
But I have also sung "Von ewiger Liebe,"
And my heart belongs to Frau Schumann's friend,
Who loved coffee and beer and outscored death.

To Cross a Bridge Half-shrouded in Mist

A colossal bridge vanishing in the mist
Spans the bay and its behemoths of ships
But dissolves in the middle—a plan imperfect
That hangs like doom from an immortal's grip.

The closer I draw the more I shudder
Just because I know it's the weather's trick—
Take away that knowledge, my heart would race
To observe the gods my spirit senses.

But what if my knowledge is just more weather
Grayer and trickier than the most threatening storm?
If I saw surfaces with perfect love,
Would I bridge the cross to the mystery I missed?

Folding

The image in my mind that still I touch,
Like years of weeping salt never so white,
Moves unmoving through memory to clutch
Your beauty to my breast of burning night.

The primal emptiness desire provokes
The silent cry every lover senses
Toiling in the embrace which never yokes
More than the flesh which owns no defenses.

The sweet-mingling fluids, by nature life,
So far beneath the threshold of spirit,
Mock our consciousness with familiar strife—
Though we would speak, we can never hear it.

Side by side in trembling completion,
We know we do not know what each other felt,
But a music beyond choosing heals the lesion,
If we let it, by folding the hands we were dealt.

Left Leg

Gnawing
and licking
before night
and temperature
fall
the chemistry
of his brain
numbing
the pain
at last
he's through
and he
hobbles
away
alive
and
free

Betrayal

You have no idea till it happens to you.

That part inside you no longer answers.
Call as you will—cry! Silence is all you hear.

Without your knowing (much less believing),
Suddenly who you were is blank, and life,
Or what you thought was life, is vacancy—
But not empty: it is full of nothing.

You serve your nothing, monster that it is,
A knot in your heart—a phantom troth-plight

To one you did not choose and never knew.

The Murdered Mother is Buried under an Avalanche of Obelisks

Who doubts the sufferings mothers endure? Their bodies bond.
If you don't understand this, you must start all over again.
Watch any mammal lick her newborn clean of the fluids and
      the debris:
In only minutes, she will remember her newborn's odor for as
      long as they live together.
Watch a newborn human fasten on the nipple: try to under-
      stand what you are seeing.
Why is it so difficult? This came out of that. (And your orgasm
      spikes your oxytocin.)
No matter how big or strong or mean you get, this does not
      change: you came out of her.
Is it any wonder men abuse women the way they do?
Have you ever heard her cry, when she thinks no one's around?
      That's the sound of life.
Who do you think you are? No matter how big or strong or
      mean you get?
You will never bury her so deep you or the world will forget
      where you came from.
Be assured no religion on earth can justify what you are doing.
      Stop deceiving yourself.
It's not her fault you think it's her fault. That's just your vanity
      patting your ass.
Under all that weight you pretend did not hurt her—she hardly
      mattered anyway—
She still reaches you. That is what *mother* means. It's time you
      learned to talk.

Shoelaces

Grandma "Soodie" taught me how to tie them.
I remember the struggle precisely.
Henry Lee didn't want me to try him,
And Alma's moods were so often icy.

The odor of her snuff and her yellowed nails
Repelled me—as if from an alien world
(Where boys are punished with dragon tails
That scrape your stomach till it heaves and hurls),

But the moment I sat down beside her
And felt her wrinkled warmth envelop me,
I trusted her for a heart so tender
That, to this day, I hear her within me,

"This way, son, you can do it, now, I'm sure."
So I keep trying, the child she made endure.

The Seven Medley Friends of Bread

BARED for you here,
each of us speaks
his idiolect,
his share of sound
and the sound of his share
as it is sheared
and sliced
to its meaning—*fragment*—
of the loaf that is shared.

DARE you think about bread?
Heat of the sun palatable,
eaten everywhere,
energy stored from so far away,
the dare of life
and the history of the world—

can you READ this story?
Yes, if your belly's full,
full of bread to store
your sinews and your nerves
against the horror,
the horror of horrors,
the hoarding of bread.

There are men who DEBAR
women and children
the poor and the halt
the blind and the weak
the black and the red
the yellow and the white

the toothless and the unwashed
the sobbing and the moaning
from bread:
that they may not eat.

To life so DEAR
each religion must borrow it
(*the* lone word of loan-words)
to figure its promises
translate its heaven
excuse its avarice
(prettify its lust),
justify the lashes
it swears
justify the body
in the eyes of god—
this body of bread
the bread of this body
(do this in remembrance).

Fields of wheat,
each BEARD aflame in the sun,
await the harvest scythe,
and the people rejoice,
the people give thanks,
the people embrace,
elders and children
and fertile, erotic bodies
of men and women;
and their gratitude
is the staff of the tyrant's scorn,
the stuff of the miser's mockery,
the never-ending parturition
of power's pleasure in penury—
scarcity
and the scare and the scar

of hunger:
the word to *starve* is the word to *die*
(*sterben*),
stiffened and stubbled,
the beard of corpses
across the face of the planet
which human eyes cannot endure.

I am not DEBRA,
no Judge I,
driving the stake through Sisera's head.
I am bread,
the bread of life,
and this I tell you—listen to me—
only when everyone living
feeds on me
will freedom and peace
grow in the world
and the earth once more
be our Mother, our Lady,
our Lady Mother:
hlǣfdige—"bread kneader,"
former of the loaf,
builder of the world,
shaper of the word.

Old English hlǣfdige *("kneader of the loaf") is the etymology of Modern English "lady."*

The Sublime Humane

I

The mountain rises, the ancient threat
As voluble now as eons ago it was
When men had no option but to ascend.

Just so, the nearer the traveler comes
The clearer the paths of shepherds and flocks,
The ascent by both already marked for all.

The idea of the mountain is complex,
As chaotic as the theory of rocks
Or as sharp as the edge that amputates

(A man must decide to lie or to fall).
The mountain does not belong to philosophers
Nor, for that matter, to shepherds and flocks:

The mountain insists on our mutual
Geography exact in inexactitude—
Call it the idea of the sublime humane.

II

Let us go you and I to the knot
Of stones massed and tumbled at the bottom
Of the gorge where the river emerges

And gaze on the bones of our cryptic dam,
How they—eroded blood-red—remind us of
The pain that pleasure composes us of

As we learn to torture the sheerest nerve
For what we believe only we should have,
No matter the moan that mourns our murder—

We will not obey what we cannot hear,
And we close our ears to the earth's tears,
And we laugh at them who love her living,

As if our flesh were anything other
Than rot of her jungles from time so vast
They mock our machines for the mimics they are.

III

Mighty are the instruments our fear constructs
To destroy, to maim, to glorify greed.
Turn the other cheek—slash it you they will.

Hidden remain the earth's secrets (and gnomes—
Is *radio* a better "gname" than *ether*?).
For each one we pry from her, one hundred

Retreat in the wake of the damage we wreak.
Like religion, science also will fail—
Government, too. All fear the fabling flesh.

IV

> *Within the infant rind of this small flower*
> *Poison hath residence and medicine power:*
> *For this, being smelt, with that part cheers each part;*
> *Being tasted, slays all senses with the heart.*
> —*Shakespeare*

Exempli gratia. Reptile venom
Hisses a fable hard to forget
And even harder (for some) to credit:

The very toxin that in one form kills me
In another conquers mortal diseases—
Flowing without is flowing within ... me.

This it is that terrifies humankind:
Life is flow, and, flowing, my life is flown,
Irreversibly, to stories I do not own.

V

Therefore let this be a promise we make
(A promise is an I-land in the flow):
We will steer ourselves but not stop the flow.

From the mountain mutually we sense
The sublime humane: even rock is flow,
Magma so hot continents melt and shift,

Flowing to pose histories yet unknown.
No Romantic ideal is the sublime
Humane but uttermost flesh and blood,

Resolved to make of, and on, the earth a world ...
The earth may waste in the blink of an eye
(*Vitaque mancipio nulli datur, omnibus usu:*

"To no one is life free; to everyone, loaned").
Therefore should the sublime humane this too avow:
If one, then all, begin this life indebted

Without the means of ever requiting
The origin from which we each derive
The energy of which desire is all.

Operatic Labor

downstage right
isolated by the spot
in a crouch
eons of hominid females
have squatted in
so compressed her diaphragm
improbably she still sings
as pure as birdsong
the morning sun greeting
her billowing skirts
revealing as much as they conceal
easy to imagine
the pelvis open wide
buttocks resting on heels
no fetus though
finds its way forward
to our stage of pain and light
yet birth there is
like all birth bestial beautiful and bloody
though we never see a drop
we hear instead
transmuted liquid
flowing through the other lips
both pairs now so close

life finds a different entry
we acknowledge this life
our birthright
we too are animals who sing
as her voice connects us to her
in her we are made singers ourselves
we assent
to the plurisingular gasp
that calls the curtain
on the changelessly changing score

Annabelle

I was barely nineteen when I found the note
tucked into the pocket of my jacket
hanging outside the biology lab.
I still see the blue ink and the pixie hand
that made every letter pirouette
in a mischievous ballet just for me:
"I want you to know I think a lot about you.
Would you like to get together some time?"
I started to dance myself that day
and, I suppose, part of me dances still
since I learned from her the consummate step:
she by grace of her favor to lead leads me
in the body I will never understand.

Michelangelo's *Florentine Pietà*

The exquisite emboldens the spirit.

Every mark of the chisel bespeaks
The master's hand, unerring eye, grim smile
At his ambition (otherwise corrosive,
Marring the mystery that masters the mar
In the marble reluctant to bare its life).

Where in the formless is the form if not
In the mind that already quarrels with
What it alone has seen?

My words are gone out.

Imperfection is an imperious mistress:
We shall call her Dame Deformity.

If Bing-a-boc is nominated imperfect,
With Boc-a-bing, she argues, we must
Already be intimate—nothing less.

The challenge is to learn, without curse
Or cruelty or cant, how Boc-a-bing
And we failed to respect each other
In the dance of adequation, the reel
In which we suppose and pose the perfect
(We must agree on a mutual fiction),
For peace surpasses perfection in time
Even when our fictions must be revised
To give credit where credit is you.

But many disdain Dame Deformity
And refuse to listen to her wisdom.

For them perfection is pretense to war,
Excuse religious or political
(Though always, at bottom, economic)
To murder men and women by the millions.
And so we cannot decide: the body
Of Jesus limp and broken or the face
Imponderably serene in sorrow
Of Nicodemus. No chisel for this.

Perhaps himself will guide us, the ugly
Florentine.

       Him Dame Deformity acknowledges
Her own, grave witness.

                    Foul-smelling, unkempt,
To life in squalor daily indifferent,
Wealthy one moment, stolen from the next,
Queer, enthralled by the human body, male
Beauty his deepest delirium, he
Consciously made good our corruption, to give
Of his vision until giving was done—
So we might choose to see.

                  In his mirror
Appalled (look again at Bartholomew's hide),
What could he do but shape an art as full
Of strange excess as he himself was full of
Suffering, that the strange excess of suffering
Might not cease to mirror how ugly we are?

Sistine Sex

L'anima che non sogna,
non pecca amar le cose di natura,
usando peso, termine e misura. *
　　　　　　—Michelangelo Buonarroti

Hard not to notice (talk about the love
Dare not mention its name!) buttocks everywhere—
Not to mention biceps, breasts, or thighs,
All more or less covered, of course (some much less),
Testifying, perhaps, to a belief
Not customary in a religion
Of surreptitious sexuality.
In his own likeness God created them,
Male and female created he them.
What more pious, then, for the master's art
Than to liken God to the likeness he blest,
His son and his saints in human posture?

*"The soul that is not dreaming does not sin to love the things of nature,
    employing weight, limit, and measure."*

Mantle

He chose his own wood from the stock to hand.
He studied the grain and eyed every warp.
He also listened how the wood might hum,
And for its song an ugly board would do
Since he could mill it to match its music.
His saws were primitive and not many,
But he kept them oiled and sharp and true,
Their bite clean and their throatiness warm.
The lathe was old and raised a hoary racket,
But he made sure it was always balanced
For turning and knurling he loved to do.
His chisels seemed to grow out of his hands
And he always carved less to coax out more.
The way he sanded his shapes one by one
Might teach the pious what patience means.
And a fit never forced made edges speak
Of measurement mastered in flesh and bone.
Long since departed, and, with him, his craft,
He never saw computers calculate
Tolerances for robotic arms,
Never saw a laser guide a cutter.
But I can remember going with him
To install the mantle in its buyer's home
And the light in his eyes at what he had made.

Duchess

Poetry descends to ordinariness
as if the resigned
were the last people on earth.
I am 60 years old, tired
of resignation and ordinariness.

Duchess was my first dog.
I will tell you about her
and maybe
you'll see what I mean.

A Cocker Spaniel
obsidian black,
excellent in form
her entire length,
she arrived
a present from an uncle
(his marriage no good,
the dog had to go),
and she was intelligent
with that intelligence
a dog will surprise you with:
from feelings to responses
instant and appropriate
to the moment
with a preciseness
that halts you
right there, right then,
to look at the dog and wonder,
how can this be?
(I know people will tell you

it's just your imagination—
if only they knew
what they were saying.)

We were dirt poor,
lived in company shacks,
but my father,
not yet the drunk he was to be,
decided to build a pen
for Duchess;
he was a carpenter,
mantle-maker for the company,
and built it on a Saturday—
2 x 4's,
chicken-coop wire,
scrap roofing metal—
I remember my awe
at its size,
watching my father stand
in what he had built
with his own two hands
in just one day.

I played with Duchess
inside her pen
down in the dirt and straw;
sometimes when it rained
we'd listen to the drops
staccato the roof,
and I'd sing to her,
her head in my lap,
her tail curling calmly,
no matter how loudly
I affronted the thunder.

I remember her coat
in my fingertips:
waves in such profusion
you could barely reach her skin,
and if you did,
she might yelp,
you pulled it that hard,
but, bunched in my hands
like clouds of softness
it pleased me so,
I can close my eyes
and knead it again,
lost in the blackness
that never let me down.

We lived together
almost a year;
I must have sung her
a thousand songs,
and she never complained,
never hid,
always cried with joy
when I came to play
and quivered,
that way a dog will quiver,
as if her whole body
were in love with me.

I was seven years old
when I lost her:
someone opened the gate,
and she ran away;
I cried, as a child will,
inconsolably,
till my father threatened me
with his belt
if I didn't shut up.

 A day or two later,
I was playing outside—
I remember the sun,
how orange hot it was—
when I looked down the hill
over the dirt road:
in the scraggly green
by the rusted hoods,
discarded drums,
forgotten vanities,
Duchess was fleeing
(you have to understand
only she could be
so pure a streak,
so sudden a slash of ink
signing the summer
shimmering
black),
and I cried out her name
over and over
till I was so hoarse
I lost my voice,
but she never stopped,
she never turned,
and I never cried
for her again
until today.

My Corgi *Shandy*

Come nine o'clock when I lie down to sleep
My Corgi *Shandy* nuzzles me "good night."
She trots to my bedside and lifts her head.
I reach down to rub it and also her ears—
Very important, her ears—and she is still
That way only a dog can be still: you feel
More than see the poise, concentration,
As only a creature of the wild,
Accustomed daily to death and hunger,
Can concentrate, always about to lunge....

When she is satisfied we have honored
The nature we share years without number
She returns to her corner in the hall
Where she keeps her vigil throughout the night
And soon I hear her breathing now and then
Broken by a whimper as she dreams I
Imagine of a vale I too might know
Where a predator springs a moment too
Late and once again we laugh in pleasure
Death cannot feel because it is not life.

The Nib of the Fountain Pen With Which He Wrote his First Love-Poem

By the vent hole in the nib of my pen
(air must rise when liquid falls), I flow
ink onto paper, the lines of my poems
witnesses to an ancient physics
of velleity, vellum, and venom—
the future's scriptural materials:
after the machines have drunk the fuels
and mutations have altered hand and eye,
the touch from tail to shoulders to tines
sends signals to neurons hitherto dormant
(despite millenniums of writing)
that now awake tell stories once ineffable,
which soak the surface with prodigious lines—
delicately erect minuscule ductus:
calligraphy at last worthy of the name,
"beautiful strokes" that remember the body
in a time when the body still belonged
to the paleography of pleasure
deciphering the scripts of ecstasy
with point and slit that weep the stain sublime.

Anatomy of Sartorial Eros,
Or the Pursuit of Pleasure

> *The* Sartorius *is the longest muscle in the human body, forming*
> *part of the quadriceps. Its name derives from the Latin for* tailor
> *which derives from a verb meaning to* repair *or* patch.
> *Sometimes it is called "the tailor's muscle."*

Put your finger, your index finger,
on your partner's hip,
edge of the blade, there,
along the iliac crest,
and trace toward her sex
(remembering to stay proud of it, though)
down the quadriceps to the knee
just above the tibia:
that is the muscle *sartorial*,
the "tailor's" indent, the long seam,
or ribbon, which, with its mate,
suggests the triangle, her legs closed,
that discovers the portal to her sex
when her legs lift and part;
put your fingertip to her lips now,
while she is looking at you,
her tongue waiting, too,
and moisten the pen copiously,
to pattern the suit of amor
the two of you are about to cut out.

When Love Is

If you ask me what love is,
Like most people,
I'll stare back at you blankly, "Huh?"
And if I do say anything,
I'll only succeed in making a fool of myself.

But if you ask me *when* love is …

> When just by her side I feel almost united …
> When the noise of the world recedes …
> When everyone I see smiles at me …
> When children I meet want me to pick them up and hold them …
> When I wake up seven hours later ready for launch, wherever …
> When even cynicism rolls off my back to the nearest gutter …
> When every woman I see radiates life to me …
> When one glass of wine makes a meal a feast …
> When her touch is enough …

Dr. Cyn Icks: A Rebuttal

You're never wrong, Dr. Icks (though, in fact,
Never more than half-right, either),
And everyone knows what a mistake it is,
Love is so wearying as well as disillusioning.

And yet, like a piano in the sky
Played by rippling rainbow fingers,
Love is always happening, happiness
Answering no question, least of all why.

A fingertip strokes the beloved's breast
Leaving no more than a trace of rose
(Such as an angel wings to a wisp of grace),
But even in a scar so slight as this

Memory still deciphers the lures
(Love's higher glyphs) to which our hearts
Stoop at speeds unimaginable but real,
So real we wonder we were ever two

And pray each other shall never sunder
Since only we speak each other's argot
And only we are got by our rule of rhyme,
That division is a ruse of history

It is our distinction to muse together,
Lest time refuse to tune into space
To resign its foolery (and revenges)
For the cosmic festival, the endless

Maintenant of the *jeu d'esprit*
That is the very vocable of love:
Holding her hand and feeling her touch
Soft on my wrist as zephyrs in a dream,

We breathe in the plenum of here and now
(Scandalized, Dr. Icks dismisses school)—
Be-Thou me as I be-I thee and We
Shall play, love's linguists, in this script of Ours.

When You Wish You Had

Everyone is an I-land.

The sun rises still though my beloved
Is gone. My incredulity halts it not.
Nor for a moment for me does life stop.

Everywhere women and men carry on
Coupling and birthing, betraying and weeping,
As if incapable of finding the cause.

Have they no feeling for the fissure in time?
Can they not hear, at the crack in space,
The peremptory howl of disbelief?

Intolerable the postulate
Of usualness…. Weep with me, you, all—
The day will come when you wish you had.

My Mother, Violets, and I

One particular bank draped in violets,
At the edge of the woods bordering the lot
Where the line of company shacks plodded on,
Paraded so many I was too young
To count them all, though some mornings I tried.

But I'd soon lie flat on my front—my shirt
Soaked to the skin with dew and cool and stained—
Picking handfuls without stepping on them,
Always watching for snakes, as I was taught,
Though I never saw one in all those summers.

I would fetch the bouquet of violets
To the back door and clamber up the stairs
Careful to protect the precious passion—
My mother would smile, then turn her head.
It did not take long to learn of her tears.

Vacation Bible School 1952

The schedule called for cutouts
to be the highlight
of the week for mothers
to view and praise.

We had learned to fold the paper
so that we could cut it
with our children's scissors
revealing our shapes.

Like most of the boys I chose the tree,
green construction paper
creased how they showed us—
a paper pine tree.

On the church patio in the sun,
laughing and poking
we lined up by our mothers
to display our art.

I could feel my mother shake
as the lady whispered.
I smell her perfume.
I see her rings.

A minute later her son tore
my pine out of my hand.
I cried as he laughed
fearless of scolding.

The other boys all sniggered
as we fumbled away—
my eyes suddenly dry
for she was crying now.

Try to Imagine a Woman's Body

Try to imagine a woman's body
Without the abuse she normally suffers—

No porn, no fists in the face, no drunken rapes.
Look at her as what she is, different from you.

We've borne side by side so long we've forgot
How unnatural the erotic is.

Habit inures us to the sexual fix:
We mate, then murder the fruit of her womb

Like all the beasts whose males eat their young
(Though we prettify ours in the name of war).

And the woman who refuses to submit?
We have a name for her, you guessed it,

"*Un*natural," she, who won't enslave herself
To a law she doesn't have to obey.

Nature doesn't give a damn about freedom—
Freedom's a game men invent to break the rules.

Nature everywhere insists, own your risk
(It's death to pretend it doesn't exist):

Men murder gods as well as their children—
If you don't believe me, ask her…if you dare.

Taste

"On my experience, Adam, freely taste,
And fear of Death deliver to the Windes."
Paradise Lost 9.988-89

Can there be a tyranny more intimate?
Its dictates do any of us deny?

Where do tongues not go, if taste entices?
The promise of sweetness seduces.

Remember, not sight nor even scent
But taste relieved you and taught you the truth

You could not otherwise admit to yourself:
Predator and prey united forever,

Ecstasy or kill, you never forget
In your mouth the serpent that forks your rapture—

Do we not, after all, taste our freedom?
For that matter, taste … the body of god …

Rose-Leaf Necklaces

We live under the tyranny of belief,
Forgetting "lief" means what we happen to "like."

We murder in the name of god-This or god-That
And drink the victims' blood as if it were wine.
We torture the earth to wring from her wealth
That misers hoard up to torture the poor.

Raindrops on rose-leaves drape necklaces
So fragile, a breath can shatter their pearls,
But hearts are heavy with heaven's weeping
Long before our clay confesses our malice
Since there can be no mistaking beauty
For any of its copies—beauty
Is the necklace that does not bind or clasp,
Revealing itself by fading at last.

Flowering Aloe

I threw the plant away end of last season
Over by the hedges of Ligustrum—
Worked loose from the soil, it had rolled over.

I wasn't upset. Its pups were everywhere:
I figured it had lived its life, made its mark—
And left the hummingbirds in very good shape.

This morning I noticed it, first time in months,
Shining green, bigger than I remembered.
I bent to pick it up, but it wouldn't budge.

My people (as we say) were German, *Schweizer*
On my mother's, *Schwarzwälder* on my father's, side—
Some fought the British in the War of Independence.

They had left to escape the Wars of Religion,
Abandoning farms, and at least one bakery,
To cross the Atlantic to face the unknown.

I've seen photos of some, haggard, but still stern,
Eyes so blue in skin so pale you'd think the sun
Had envied their faces some primal fire,

The passion that drove down their roots, perhaps—
Americans now, errantly flowering
Wherever some other ground would allow.

Luck

I used up all my luck by age twenty-five.
I remember old men who spoke of luck:
"You only get so much and then you're done."
I was so young—I didn't believe them.
I thought you made your own luck, "like a man,"
but that's only a TV commercial:
no one can "make" luck—cancer's always waiting,
or some hot bod' ready to take it all.
I've lived forty years now without any luck,
limping through history like everyone else,
but I've learned a thing or two, even so,
because I've had my eyes and ears open
most of the time. People with no luck,
which is 'most everyone, do weird things:
their kids are maybe alcoholics,
so they smile and pour a few more drinks,
or their parents dying exhaust the savings,
so they suit up and sign another note,
or they're so starved for sex, they lie awake
crying and hugging their knees damaged by jogging
(no fun in the manner of Fido for them).
Thus, I conclude, luck is not what we think.
Luck is not possessions, which, anyway,
only possess you, feasting on your greed.
Luck is the gift of freedom from tomorrow,
time off from winding yesterday's clock,
the minute you feel today is your own
singing to yourself how lucky you are.

The Heart of Poetry

For Robert B. Shaw

Poetry and we parted long ago
When we concluded that we cannot earn
A living from what in our hearts we know
We could learn of living if hearts got a turn.

But a turn is a contested choice
And some will scoff at the use of the word.
Others will laugh and sneer at the voice
That pulpits ideals they swear are absurd.

But their boast is more naïve than the dream
Of a world where people don't hoard but share;
Where cadence and rhyme are held in esteem
As measures of imagination to spare—

The kindness of the kin who ken they can
Return the heart of poetry to man.

Acknowledgments

I recognize and honor the following—

Robert B. Shaw for his graciousness and professionalism over these many years …

Robert Morgan who long ago took a young man's poems seriously …

Edwin G. Wilson, a model to me of a life in letters for more than forty years now …

The late Judson Allen who taught me that love and language are needful to each other …

The late Julian Wasserman from whom I learned what a sense of humor really is …

The founders of <u>bestthinking.com</u> who have published my work in the name of best thinking …

John Summerfield, sometime my student, now my publisher, and always in my experience a good man …

My family—Judy, Brian, Michelle, Oliver, Elaine— without whom nothing …

www.ingramcontent.com/pod-product-compliance
Lightning Source LLC
LaVergne TN
LVHW021545080426
835509LV00019B/2849